Dealing with Drugs

Marijuana

Troon Harrison Adams

Crabtree Publishing Company
www.crabtreebooks.com

Developed and produced by: Plan B Book Packagers
www.planbbookpackagers.com

Editorial director: Ellen Rodger

Art director: Rosie Gowsell-Pattison

Editor: Molly Aloian

Proofreader: Wendy Scavuzzo

Cover design: Margaret Amy Salter

Project coordinator: Kathy Middleton

**Production coordinator and
   prepress technician:** Katherine Berti

Print coordinator: Katherine Berti

Photographs:
Front cover: Photos.com/Mike Cherim;
Title page: Diego Cervo/Shutterstock.com; p. 6:
mojito.mak[dog]gmail.com/Shutterstock.com;
p. 8: Maka/Shutterstock.com; p. 9: Eric Gevaert/
Shutterstock.com; p. 11: Juan Camilo Berna/
Shutterstock.com; p. 12: Sergei Bachlakov/
Shutterstock.com; p. 13: Linday Lohan LPJ /
Shutterstock.com; p. 14: JustASC / Shutterstock.com;
p. 15: Library of Congress Prints and Photographs
Division, New York World-Telegram and the Sun
Newspaper Photograph Collection. p. 16: Lucian
Coman/Shutterstock.com; p. 17: Kato Inowe/
Shutterstock.com; p. 18: Kolosigor/Shutterstock.com;
p. 20: fusebulb/Shutterstock.com; p. 21: CLIPAREA l
Custom media/Shutterstock.com; p. 22: Jiri
Sebesta/Shutterstock.com; p. 23: dubassy/
Shutterstock.com; p. 24: Sergei Bachlakov/
Shutterstock.com; p. 25: Area Shot/Shutterstock.com;
p. 26: Nicholas Belton/Shutterstock.com; p. 28:
Kailash K Soni/Shutterstock.com; p. 31: Frontpage/
Shutterstock.com; p. 32: Couperfield/Shutterstock.com;
p. 35: Coka/Shutterstock.com; p. 36: Eric Gevaert/
Shutterstock.com; p. 37: Sergei Bachlakov/
Shutterstock.com; p. 38: Santiago Cornejo/

Library and Archives Canada Cataloguing in Publication

Harrison, Troon, 1958-
   Marijuana / Troon Harrison Adams.

(Dealing with drugs)
Includes index.
Issued also in electronic formats.
ISBN 978-0-7787-5509-8 (bound).--ISBN 978-0-7787-5516-6 (pbk.)

   1. Marijuana--Juvenile literature. 2. Marijuana--Therapeutic
use--Juvenile literature. 3. Marijuana abuse--Juvenile literature.
I. Title. II. Series: Dealing with drugs (St. Catharines, Ont.)

HV5822.M3A33 2011   j362.29'5   C2011-907351-X

Library of Congress Cataloging-in-Publication Data

Adams, Troon Harrison.
   Marijuana / Troon Harrison Adams.
      p. cm. -- (Dealing with drugs)
   Includes index.
   ISBN 978-0-7787-5509-8 (reinforced library binding : alk. paper)
-- ISBN 978-0-7787-5516-6 (pbk. : alk. paper) -- ISBN 978-1-4271-
8824-3 (electronic pdf) -- ISBN 978-1-4271-9727-6 (electronic
html)
   1. Marijuana--Juvenile literature. 2. Marijuana--Therapeutic
use--Juvenile literature. 3. Marijuana abuse--Juvenile literature.
I. Title.

HV5822.M3.A243 2012
362.29'5--dc23
                                                    2011044840

Crabtree Publishing Company

www.crabtreebooks.com   1-800-387-7650

Printed in the U.S.A./112011/JA20111018

**Published in Canada
Crabtree Publishing**
616 Welland Ave.
St. Catharines, Ontario
L2M 5V6

**Published in the United States
Crabtree Publishing**
PMB 59051
350 Fifth Avenue, 59th Floor
New York, New York 10118

**Published in the United Kingdom
Crabtree Publishing**
Maritime House
Basin Road North, Hove
BN41 1WR

**Published in Australia
Crabtree Publishing**
3 Charles Street
Coburg North
VIC 3058

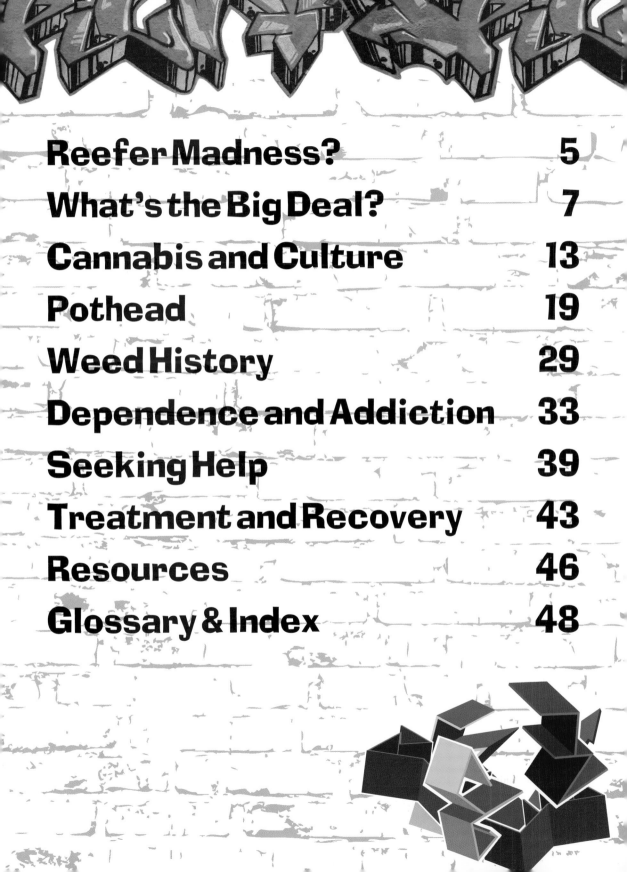

Facts & Stats

 Marijuana is the most commonly used illicit drug in the world. An annual survey called *Monitoring the Future* reports that 85 percent of American high school seniors say marijuana is "easy to obtain."

 The Drug Abuse Warning Network (DAWN) estimated that marijuana was a factor in over 374,000 emergency department visits in the United States in 2008.

The weight of marijuana for sale can be increased by the secret addition of lead, glass particles, turpentine, boot polish, engine oil, glue, or animal feces.

 Marijuana's active ingredient, THC, is stored in fatty tissue. Traces of it can still be detected in drug testing weeks after it has been smoked.

Introduction
Reefer Madness?

Perhaps you've laughed at movie actors getting stoned and acting weird in the movies. You might hear musicians praising the pleasures of pot. Maybe someone at school has offered to sell you marijuana. At parties, your friends might light up a joint and tell you that smoking pot is relaxing and harmless. Peer pressure can be tough to withstand. You'd like to fit in, be cool, and have fun too. Maybe your friends are right and smoking pot is a risk-free way to chill out. After all, marijuana is natural—it comes from a plant, right?

Marijuana is a plant, but even natural substances can contain potent chemicals that alter the **molecular** balance of your body and brain. Many legal medications, available by prescription, have been developed from natural substances. Plant **compounds** can be potent and toxic. Just because something is natural doesn't mean that it's safe or harmless—or nonaddictive.

Marijuana, like all mind-altering substances, is illegal to use recreationally and can do harm. In this book, you'll learn how marijuana affects the body, how it can be addictive, and how any addiction is dangerous.

Chapter 1
What's the Big Deal?

Pot, weed, ganja, herb, wacky tobaccy, dagga, grass, esra, reefer, bhang, boom...the slang names for marijuana are endless. Marijuana may have many names but it is one thing: the dried leaves, stems and flowers of the cannabis plant. It is used to get high. Marijuana is smoked in cigarettes, often called joints, or in pipes. It is also inhaled as vapors. Cannabis can be processed into powder form and pressed into bricks or cakes. The buds of the cannabis plant can be compressed to collect the resin and oils called hashish or hash. Hash is also smoked for a powerful high.

Marijuana and hashish have been around for a long time. Like many illicit, or illegal drugs today, they were once legal. Pot has a **mystique** that has made it appealing to many people. It is often thought of as a "soft" drug that does little or no harm and that it is "no big deal." After all, even prominent politicians have smoked it and it hasn't hurt them, right? Research shows that even casual use can make it hard for users to think clearly, and can harm memory and the ability to learn. Regular use can lead to psychosis, a severe mental disorder, in some people.

The Plant

Different species of cannabis grow wild in Central Asia, South Asia, and Central Russia. The plants are wind pollinated. *Cannabis sativa* can grow up to 14 feet (4 meters) tall in warm, lowland regions. The shorter and bushier *Cannabis indica* is suited to higher, colder places. Wild marijuana can be found growing on the sides of roads throughout Asia. Some of these wild plants are relatively mild if consumed, as they have not been **cultivated** to make them more potent. Cannabis plants have been used for thousands of years for **hemp fiber**, nutritious hemp seeds, religious rituals, and recreation. It has also been used in some cultures for its pain killing properties—with people ingesting it in foods or chewing the milder leaves, which contain less mind-altering chemicals. Archaeologists have even found cannabis in the 2,700 year old grave of a **shaman** in China.

Industrial hemp is grown for its fiberous stalks, which can be used to make rope and fabric. Hemp was once a widely-grown plant.

Pot in the Schoolyard

Okay, so we know that cannabis is a plant that grows wild in some areas of the world. It is also a multi-million dollar worldwide industry. Marijuana grown **commercially** today is pretty powerful stuff. The "weed" that someone might offer to sell you at school will be grey, green, or brownish in color. It will look like a bag of dried leaves and is likely to smell strongly. This cannabis, harvested from cultivated female plants, contains 400 different chemicals. These chemicals change your brain function, affect your organs and hormones, and alter your body's ability to grow, respond, develop, and heal.

THC Rising

One chemical found in cannabis is mainly responsible for giving users a high. It is 9-tetrahydrocannabinol or THC. Due to the presence of this chemical, and of other **cannabinoids**, marijuana is classed as a psychoactive drug. Psychoactive drugs contain substances that alter how the brain functions and how the body's **nervous system** works. They make you feel different, respond differently, and perceive things differently than you normally would. The percentage of THC in marijuana varies from one to 20 percent or higher. The average amount of THC in plants is rising as growers try to provide buyers with a stronger high. It is estimated that the average level of THC has doubled since 1998.

Legit Uses

Many psychoactive drugs are legal with a doctor's prescription and are used to treat specific health problems. They are **derived** from plant sources that are illegal to grow or sell as recreational drugs. For example, cocaine, a stimulant made from the coca plant, is used legally in **anaesthetics** administered in hospitals and doctor's offices. Marijuana compounds (the chemical substances or elements in the plant) are used in several legal prescription drugs in the United States and Canada. The drugs treat nausea in cancer patients and pain from other diseases.

Medical Marijuana

Medical marijuana is the term used to describe cannabis that is used legally for medical purposes in some U.S. states and provinces of Canada. With a doctor's prescription, users can buy or, in some cases, grow, marijuana to treat illnesses. The marijuana is sold in legal clinics, or smoked openly at compassion clubs. Compassion clubs are groups that allow those with prescriptions to smoke or eat the drug together. Medical marijuana is considered **controversial**, as many people believe illnesses can be treated with other prescription drugs.

Stoners and Tokers

On the street, marijuana users are known as stoners, bakers, potheads, or tokers. The terms refer to the fact marijuana gets them high, or "stoned" and smoking a joint is sometimes called toking.

On the Street

Cannabis that is grown and sold illegally is sometimes considered a "soft" street drug. The "soft" term comes from the fact that many people think it isn't as addictive or harmful as other "hard" drugs. The problem is, the drug trade—including marijuana—is dominated by drug gangs or **cartels**. These gangs don't want one time, or casual users. They want steady customers to bring in increasing profits. They count on people developing dependencies on the drugs they sell. There's no telling what goes into the marijuana sold on the street or through dealers. The pot is sometimes laced with other more powerful drugs such as **PCP** or cocaine. These drugs intensify the high and make users more dependant.

In the United States, cannabis is classified as a Schedule I drug. This means it has a high potential for abuse. Each state also has its own laws that outlaw marijuana cultivation, selling, or possession for recreational use. In Canada, it has been a criminal act to grow, sell, or possess marijuana since the Opium and Drug Act of 1923.

Marijuana is legal for medical use—with a doctor's prescription in several U.S. states.

Chapter 2
Cannabis and Culture

It's the weekend and you're hanging out with friends, chowing down pizza and watching a movie called *Pineapple Express*. It's about a rare strain of pot and a lot of the characters are smoking, including school kids. Stoner movies have been popular for decades. They are often comedies that make drug use look amusing. In fact, pop culture is full of references on marijuana smoking and growing. From music to magazines, cannabis is often promoted and even celebrated. There is even a vocal push to legalize, or decriminalize marijuana for recreational use. Why is it that marijuana has such a big public profile?

Actress Lindsay Lohan has had a much publicized battle with drug and alcohol abuse. She has admitted to smoking pot. Celebrity stoners often make the drug more appealing to young people.

Marijuana in the Movies

Reefer Madness is a 1936 film originally produced as a way to educate parents on the dangers of cannabis use among their children. Today the film is seen as **propaganda**, because it exaggerates the effects of the drug to scare the viewer. While the intent of *Reefer Madness* was to warn about the dangers of marijuana use, many other movies make light of pot. In the 1970s, Richard "Cheech" Marin and Tommy Chong became a well-known comedy duo. They are still popular today. Their love of marijuana was no secret, and the duo released several comedy albums and films in which they portrayed spaced-out pot smokers. In 2003, Chong was sentenced to nine months in prison for possessing drug paraphernalia. Many comedies produced today feature at least some reference to smoking pot.

In movies and propaganda films, marijuana users are portrayed as either silly or crazy from using the drug.

It's All in the Name

Maui Wowi, Acapulco Gold, B.C. Bud are slang names of well-known and potent strains of cannabis.

Famous Potheads

It's fairly common nowadays to hear public figures own up to smoking marijuana when they were younger. Some claim it was a youthful mistake and others say they didn't inhale. Marijuana use has been written about in literature, and was a feature of early jazz, rock and roll, reggae, hip hop, and rap. Tobacco and marijuana were commonly smoked in jazz clubs in the 1920s and 1930s. Musicians, as well known as Louis Armstrong and Nat King Cole, referred to marijuana as jive, viper, golden leaf, and Texas tea. Reefer jazz was widely listened to by mainstream American fans. In the 1960s and 1970s, rock musicians began singing about marijuana and other illicit drugs. By the 1990s, dub music, hip hop, and rap music regularly featured songs about getting wasted on weed or how marijuana smoking "eases your mind." While some politicians, musicians, authors, and celebrities have openly admitted or even advocated the use of marijuana, not everyone is a pothead. There are many other successful public figures who have never used it and have never wanted to use it.

Legendary jazz trumpeter Louis Armstrong apparently regularly smoked marijuana and was arrested for it in 1930.

Pot and Religion?

Cannabis, like many psychoactive drugs, has been used in many religions and belief systems. It is believed to heighten spiritual experience during worship and rituals. Historians think the ancient Scythians, a people who inhabited parts of Central Asia, used marajuana vapors in their religious rituals. The ancient Vedic texts, or Hindu religious writings, of India also mention cannabis as a sacred plant. It was used at temples during festivals.

The Rastafari religious movement, which traces its beginnings to Jamaica in the 1930s, is one modern religion that makes use of cannabis. Rastas smoke "the herb" or ganja, as they call it, to bring them closer to God, whom they call Jah. Ganja is illegal in Jamaica and other countries, where Rastas live. Some of the most famous Rastas were and are reggae musicians. Reggae is a type of music that developed in Jamaica. It often praises Jah and the Rasta way of life—including smoking ganja.

Two Rasta men roll a marijuana cigarette prior to worship. In the Rastafari belief system, marijuana is believed to be the Biblical "tree of life" that brings people closer to Jah, or God.

Risky Business

Watching movies that make light of smoking marijuana and listening to music about getting high may make you feel that marijuana isn't a problem. Popular media can make illegal drug use seem appealing and harmless. This does not change the actual facts: using marijuana is a risky illegal activity with consequences, including fines, criminal records, and jail time. Whether you are a teenager or a rich, famous adult, illicit drug use can have health consequences, including addiction.

The Black Market

There's nothing amusing about the black market for drugs. Billions of dollars change hands in the process of cannabis growing, smuggling, and selling. Cannabis is estimated to be one of the highest value crops in California, New York, and Florida. Who gets to keep the big bucks? Often, its organized crime—or networks of criminal gangs. Organized crime launders money, sells weapons, and engages in human trafficking. Drugs, including cocaine, Ecstasy, heroin, and marijuana, are smuggled over international borders. Marijuana smuggling is one of the biggest money-makers for organized crime groups. Where there is organized crime, there is violence. In Mexico, between 2006 and 2010, over 28,000 people died in drug-related violence.

Chapter 3
Pothead

The effects of marijuana depend on different factors, including the amount of THC in the pot consumed. Unless tested in a lab, there is no way of knowing what this amount truly is. How the drug is "done" also affects how rapidly it is absorbed into the body. Smoking is the fastest delivery method. It rapidly passes THC from the lungs into the bloodstream, organs, and brain.

Your brain is the center for processing messages. Different parts of your brain handle messages about different things going on in your body and your environment. The brain's **cerebellum** handles messages about muscle control and coordination. In the **hippocampus**, messages about storing memories—what to remember and what to forget—are dealt with. The **amygdala** deals with messages about anxiety, fear, and emotion. All parts of the brain receive and send chemical messages. The body produces its own chemical messengers, called neurotransmitters. These transmit, or send, messages along the neurons, or nerves. There are places in the brain and organs where these transmitters are made and received. The receiving sites are called receptors.

Fooled by THC

The psychoactive, or mind-altering ingredient in marijuana, 9-tetrahydrocannabinol or THC, mimics the brain's own chemicals. Within seconds of being inhaled, THC binds onto the brain's cannabinoid receptors. Most of these receptors are located in areas that deal with pleasure, movement, coordination, memory, thinking, and **perception**. THC disrupts the brain's message system. It stimulates the brain to release a chemical messenger called dopamine. By overstimulating the receptor sites and dopamine production, THC produces sensations and feelings called a high. Being high might seem like something fun, but it means that your brain is not functioning in a normal, healthy manner. Your brain changes as a result of the flood of dopamine and your neurotransmitters make less natural dopamine. After a while, larger amounts of pot are needed to create a dopamine flood, or high—leading users to feel they "need" to smoke.

In the brain's cerebellum, THC disrupts coordination, balance, and reaction time. If you like to play sports, do gymnastics, or rollerblade for fun, you might find that smoking pot makes you drop the ball, fall off the balance beam, or trip and stumble. Your coach might lecture you to stay focused.

The hypothalamus controls appetite.

The amygdala is the area of the brain responsible for emotion, anxiety, and fear.

The hippocampus helps with memory and sequencing.

The cerebellum is the brain's center for motor control and coordination.

Slooooow Reeeaaaction

If you're old enough to drive a car, you want your reaction time and reflexes to be fully operational. Marijuana jeopardizes your ability to drive safely for up to five hours after smoking. Getting into a car stoned puts you, your buddies in the back seat, and other drivers at risk. Marijuana is the most common drug, after alcohol, found in drivers in American car accidents. Police officers are trained to recognize drivers impaired by drugs. Drivers can be required to give a sample of blood for testing. If THC shows up, the driver will be fined, charged with a criminal offense and, if convicted, given a criminal record.

Fuzzy Thinking

In the brain's hippocampus, THC changes how information is processed, stored, and retrieved. If you smoke pot, your grades might start to fall. It can become more difficult to learn new information in class, or to retrieve old information when you're writing an exam. Your parents or teachers might demand to know what's going on. THC's affects on learning can last for weeks after using marijuana, so trying to "get clean" before an important exam won't work. Using pot is related to lower grades, and lowers chances of graduating and of being employed.

Marijuana, whether inhaled through a bong (right) or consumed in other ways, makes it difficult to think and make decisions clearly.

In the Short Term

When marijuana is smoked, it affects the body and brain within minutes. The first emotional feelings might be euphoria as THC affects the amygdala. Some people feel light-headed, relaxed, giddy, and find everything funny. Other smokers don't get this affect but instead feel confused, agitated, and frightened. The physical body responds with an increased heart rate. Your pulse can surge from the normal 60 beats per minute to 160 beats, increasing the risk of heart attack. Blood vessels expanding in the eyes give them a blood-shot appearance. Overall, blood pressure drops. Hunger, dry mouth, and slurred speech might occur.

As brain function is altered, things around the smoker seem louder and brighter. Time and space seem different, and it gets harder to focus or pay attention. Memory and concentration are also altered. Finally, there are the psychomotor effects: coordination suffers so you might have difficulty operating that table saw in shop class or riding your bike safely to a buddy's place.

Marijuana often makes people hungry, which may be what makes it useful for some cancer patients suffering from nausea.

Long-Term Effects

Puffing on a fat doobie does more than make you high; it chokes your lungs. Marijuana smokers inhale three to five times more carbon monoxide than do cigarette smokers. If you play sports, pot can ruin your performance by making you wheeze and cough. Researchers in England found that smoking marijuana caused deterioration in lung function. If you want to use your muscles, keep the clean air flowing in your lungs!

Marijuana use has been shown to suppress immune system function, making it likely that you'll catch other illnesses. You might miss more classes or team events. Harmful fungus or pesticides present in some weed adds to the health risks.

Marijuana is consumed many ways, including cooked in foods. When eaten, the high is slightly delayed, but can last for hours.

Potent Weed

The THC potency of marijuana has increased over the last 30 years—making weed stronger than ever before.

Pot and Depression

Smoking pot gives you four times the risk of developing a severe depression. Research shows that adolescents who smoke marijuana weekly are three times more likely to have suicidal thoughts. By changing the brain's chemical balance, in the same way that cocaine and heroin do, marijuana makes some users feel overwhelmed by anxiety and panic. Some withdraw from friends and family. Research also shows a link between marijuana use and psychosis in some users. Psychosis is a serious condition where a person loses touch with reality, might hallucinate, hear voices, not know where they are or who they are with. Studies suggest that young marijuana users also have an increased risk of developing schizophrenia. This devastating, lifelong mental illness has no cure.

Feeling forgetful? Marijuana use interferes with a person's ability to form new memories. User also have slower reaction times, making driving dangerous.

Gateway Drug?

Some studies show that if you begin smoking marijuana in your adolescence, or early teens, you are more likely to abuse other psychoactive drugs as you grow up. Cannabis is considered to be a "gateway drug" to other substances. A gateway drug is a drug whose use can be proven to lead to the use of other drugs—with even more harmful effects. Some studies have shown that cannabis use is a predictor for future use of amphetamines or heroin. One survey of people who smoked marijuana regularly before the age of 15 found that 62 percent went on to use cocaine.

Other Risks

Abusing drugs of any kind affects your judgment. When you're high, you're not thinking clearly. You can make mistakes such as having risky sex, perhaps by failing to use condoms or by having sex very young or with multiple partners. Using drugs increases your risk of contracting sexually transmitted diseases such as herpes or HIV. Buying marijuana also puts teens at risk because they meet people involved in an illegal activity. Your local pot dealer might set you up with other drugs, or get you involved with criminals.

Marijuana advocates are arrested at a protest for possessing the drug.

Bad Trip

You might have seen the video on the web or television. It showed an obviously high music and television star Miley Cyrus talking and acting strangely. Cyrus had just turned 18 and had just smoked salvia, a legal (at the time) plant leaf. Salvia is a psychoactive plant, also called Sally D, that is dried and smoked. Its effects on the user include a distorted sense of reality, disconnection, and hallucinations. Salvia can cause a very bad trip for users. Seeing Cyrus, a high-profile role model for adolescents, talking and laughing uncontrollably, and acting high, seemed a shocking endorsement for the drug. She has since announced that smoking salvia was a bad decision and a "bad trip." Salvia isn't the only herb that can give users a "bad trip." Some users of marijuana and hashish can experience frightening and long-lasting feelings of **paranoia** after smoking up. These drugs are mood-altering. Experts advise people experiencing a bad trip to

- remind themselves that they have taken a drug and that the sensation will end and they will be okay

- focus on breathing deeply, as fear is often made worse with shallow breathing

- surround yourself with helpful, calm friends who can reassure you that the drug's effect will soon end

Chapter 4
Weed History

Cannabis, wild and cultivated, has a long history in human cultures. Central Asian shamans, or magicians and medicine men, used cannabis for thousands of years to induce **trances**. In India, as far back as 3000 B.C., cannabis was used in Hindu religious festivals as bhang, a beverage, ganja, or smoked cannabis, and hashish, or resin. The ancient Chinese manual of medicinal plants, *Classic of Materia Medica*, refers to the plant's power. It contained this information on cannabis: "To take much makes people see demons and throw themselves about like maniacs."

Ancient societies used cannabis as medicine for pain, loss of appetite, infection, convulsions, as well as diseases such as cholera, and nervous disorders. In the absence of scientific knowledge about medicine, there was a strong link between magic and healing. Plants that had magical and mind-altering properties were believed to be medicinally important as well. Cannabis first arrived in the United States as a commercial hemp crop in 1611. It was grown at the Jamestown settlement. Hemp is a plant whose sturdy stem fibers were used to make rope and other fabrics.

Marijuana as Medicine

Listed in early editions of American medical journals as a helpful herb, cannabis was used as a medicine from the 1800s to the mid-1900s. It was available as a **tincture** or a tablet to treat cough and **colic**. It was also used as a sedative and pain killer. Asthma patients were even advised to smoke it as a treatment. Women in labor were given marijuana to ease their pain. The public didn't change its mind about marijuana until the growing scourge of opium addiction in the late 1800s.

Long Arm of the Law

Opium and drugs derived from it, such as morphine and laudanum, were very popular in the 1800s. It was estimated that up to five percent of the American population was addicted to opium at the time, either from recreational use or as a medical treatment. Opium made users drowsy and inactive, or severely ill when they tried to quit. Opium's bad reputation spread to marijuana use. Marijuana use was opposed on moral grounds because it was believed habitual users were ruining themselves. Marijuana users were considered crazy when using the drug and prone to violent behavior—even when there was no proof that this was the case. Beginning in 1914, the first drug laws were introduced to regulate and control opiates and cocaine. This paved the way for other laws. The first marijuana laws were laws taxing the drug. By the 1930s, most states had laws regulating or prohibiting marijuana growth, sales, and distribution.

Controlled Substance

Although in many states, marijuana was still legal for some time—when prescribed by a doctor, governments soon yielded to public pressure. Marijuana was deemed an addictive drug by the U.S. Federal Bureau of Narcotics in the 1930s. Laws have been targetting growers, dealers, and users ever since. Today, marijuana is federally a Schedule 1 controlled substance in the U.S., meaning it is designated as having a high potential for abuse and no accepted medical use. Each state also has different marijuana laws. Some states are strict and others more lenient. Oregon, for example decriminalized the possession of small amounts of marijuana in 1973. The former governor of New Mexico even called for marijuana to be legalized in 1998. Florida law, by contrast, allows for a five-year jail sentence and a $6,000 fine for someone caught possessing one ounce of pot.

Advocates of legalizing recreational use of marijuana claim the drug isn't harmful.

Marijuana Industry

Marijuana is a multi-billion dollar industry. An estimated 22 million pounds (10 million kg) of marijuana are harvested each year in the U.S.

Chapter 5
Dependence and Addiction

Some of your friends might try to persuade you that smoking a little weed won't lead to problems. You're not going to be addicted like a heroin junkie, right? The popular belief that marijuana is not addictive is misleading. Like other drugs, cannabis can create physical and psychological **dependence**. It can be difficult to break the habit. Marijuana is one of the top drugs that youth seek help for.

How do you know if you're addicted to a substance? Sometimes, people with a habit of substance abuse deny that they have an addiction. They don't want to admit that, without the substance, they can't function in daily life. Alcohol, cigarettes, marijuana, and other illicit drugs, can all cause addiction. If you feel that you really need a joint, cannot stop thinking about it, crave it, will take risks to get it, and cannot face the day without it, then it is a safe bet to say you are dependent on marijuana.

Dependence

Studies show that long-term marijuana use can lead to addiction. Addiction happens when you have difficulty controlling your drug use. Addicts often say "I can quit when I want to." The truth is, they really can't. If you started using when you were young, it is more likely that you will become dependent on the drug. Dependence affects your body and your mind.

Physical dependence means that your body has adjusted to the effects of THC over time. If you stop suddenly, you will experience withdrawal symptoms, including irritability, aggression, and inability to sleep. You might experience increased anxiety, sweating, tremors, upset stomach, and loss of appetite. Psychological dependence means that you are used to being high, and now it's difficult to function with a healthy chemical balance. You might feel a compulsive craving for a joint and feel anxious if you don't have one.

Depression and Sadness

Other signs of addiction can include loss of interest in your activities and lack of motivation. It may seem that nothing matters anymore. You might be anxious and depressed, feeling deep and overwhelming sadness for no reason connected to daily events. In some people, this leads to thoughts of suicide. You might experience problems with failing grades at school, and difficulties with aggression and anger. You might even find it harder to persevere when you're dealing with problems. Coping with everything going on in life may become difficult and you may just want to give up.

Occasional sadness is normal. Being sad often, or all the time, particularly when connected with drug use, is not normal and requires professional help.

More Risks

Studies show chronic users of marijuana have lower grades in school and are more likely to drop out.

Needing More

Maybe you used to get a strong high from one joint. But lately, it seems that just one doesn't do much for you. You have to smoke more to get the same feelings. Or you have to find a supply of stronger marijuana, maybe skunk or netherweed. This is because your body has adjusted to the levels of THC you've been inhaling. Cannabinoids are accumulating in the membrane around your neurons. You have developed a tolerance to the drug, and you have to inhale more of it to get the same affects.

All for the Pot

Health care professionals use a reference book, *Diagnostic and Statistical Manual of Mental Disorders* (DSM-IV), that lists the symptoms of addiction. Pot smokers display all the symptoms. They develop tolerance, use marijuana even when it's causing negative side effects, give up social and recreational activities that get in the way of smoking, and experience withdrawal symptoms if they try to quit. In America in 2002, 4.3 million people were classified as dependent on marijuana. If you are a teenager who begins smoking marijuana, you have a one-in-six chance of becoming an addict.

Danger Zone

Being addicted to a drug is like handing over control over your life. Instead of trying to get good grades, or hang out with friends, all you think about is smoking your next reefer. Instead of wanting to play on the ball team, you obsess over how to find enough money to buy more grass. You're irritable and tense. Your teachers call your parents, you lose friendships, and your coach suspends you from the team. You're coughing. You're tired but not sleeping well. You take driving lessons because you want independence, but you make stupid mistakes and fail the test. You may get into fights and even consider doing a little shoplifting to finance your pot deals.

It can be hard to recognize, and easy to deny, the control marijuana has over you.

Chapter 6
Seeking Help

Quitting marijuana can be hard. Some people try several times before succeeding. Often, people who like to toke up also smoke cigarettes, drink alcohol, or use harder drugs such as Ecstasy or crack cocaine. Having multiple addictions makes quitting complicated. Compared to these other problems, smoking marijuana might seem like no big deal. However, using cannabis over time causes the same addiction patterns and difficulties as other substances. Quitting can cause withdrawal symptoms

and a sense of being overwhelmed. Social problems occur if your friendships are based on getting high. It is likely that you will lose some friends. If smoking up was the key to your friendships, they weren't there for the real you anyway.

Coming in From the Cold

Coming clean and telling the truth about a drug problem can be challenging. You may worry that you will be punished or judged. If you keep something secret, you cannot be criticized—but you cannot be helped either. Sharing the depth of your habit with a

friend, a counselor, or other trusted adult, is called disclosure. Disclosure means choosing to tell the truth about yourself. This is the first step in getting the professional help that enables you to change things. It takes courage to lay your issues out, but disclosure is a positive, empowering step. Just make sure you are ready for it. Some people may reject you, but most will want to help you.

You might be surprised who will help you when you ask them to.

In the Grip

An estimated nine to ten percent of people who use marijuana will become dependent on it. The younger a person is when they start using, the more likely it is that they will be dependent.

Helping Your Friends

Have noticed a friend or family member changing in negative ways? Do you suspect your friend needs help? The signs listed below could indicate that your friend has developed a dependence on marijuana:

- Loses interest in sports, hobbies, school events
- Chills out with new friends who use marijuana, other drugs, or alcohol
- Is aggressive, fights, gets into trouble, or steals
- Acts very anxious, in a panic, or paranoid
- Drops grades or skips classes
- Seems depressed and sad, withdrawing from friendships

If you want to help your friend, be sympathetic and avoid making accusations. Let your friend know you'll be supportive, and suggest places to find help such as free clinics or school counselors. It may be frustrating to see a friend struggling with drug dependency. They may reject your suggestions that they need professional help. Remember that you cannot bully someone into getting clean. You can only offer assistance.

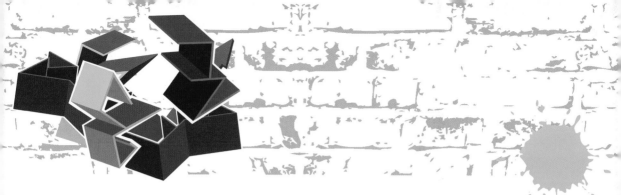

Chapter 7
Treatment and Recovery

Drug dependency and addiction are lifelong battles. Maybe you're trying for the first time to quit smoking marijuana, or maybe this is your second or third attempt. Either way, you have made a commitment to yourself to lead a healthier life. It will be a difficult fight, and you may stumble along the way.

In America in 2008, 61 percent of drug abusers under the age of 15 were trying to quit marijuana. Many users need help with quitting and turn to medical professionals, including doctors, psychiatrists, and psychologists. Trying to quit on your own can be overwhelming if you experience withdrawal symptoms, including poor sleep leading to tiredness, anxiety, depression, loneliness, and a constant craving for a toke. If your peers don't support your choice to quit, you might find yourself without friends when you need them most. This can increase feelings of isolation. Health professionals can support you, one step at a time, through the recovery process.

In Treatment

Treatment for marijuana addiction can include talk therapy where you meet with a professional trained in addiction to talk about the real reasons why you want to get wasted. You might meet in private, or in a group with other addicts. Cognitive behavioral therapy (CBT) and motivational enhancement therapy (MET) are two common drug treatments. CBT teaches you strategies for dealing with problems, and MET helps you to make fast, internally motivated changes, or changes that address your personal desires and needs. A therapist will help you deal with underlying issues, such as past trauma, that might have influenced you to abuse drugs. Treatment might be offered to your whole family to help deal with issues raised by addiction. In addition, medications may be prescribed for symptoms such as inability to sleep.

Be Kind to Yourself

The effects of marijuana withdrawal are not life-threatening. They are uncomfortable but short-lived. Most symptoms diminish in a week or two after your last smoke. During this period, eat and sleep well, and stay in close contact with supportive people. Deep breathing, yoga, or other gentle exercise, can all be calming and strengthening. You can help yourself at any time, in any place, by thinking positive. Positive self-talk includes messages such as "I can do this" or "I'm strong" and "I'm making smart choices. I'm looking forward to my future."

More Than the Blues

One withdrawal symptom that can become too severe to deal with alone is depression. Depression can be treated with medication and therapy. If you feel suicidal, do not wait to see if the feeling passes. Always get immediate help by calling a crisis line, or telling someone (such as a teacher or parent) how you're feeling. Here are some tips on how to recognize depression:

- You've had sad, hopeless feelings almost every day for two weeks
- You're losing interest in friends, school life, and other activities
- You're tired, grouchy, and not sleeping well
- You cry easily, or feel like crying but are unable to
- It's difficult to focus, or to remember things
- You want everyone to leave you alone; you just want to stay in your room
- You think it might be better to end it all by killing yourself

Relapse

Most recovering addicts relapse at least once on their road to clean living. It is important to recognize that relapse does not mean total failure. Studies show long-time users attempt to quit at least six times before succeeding.

Resources

The Internet is crowded with sites about smoking weed, but many advocate its use and they don't all give accurate or unbiased facts. Visit your library for books that contain factual information, and look for websites that offer support that is nonjudgmental. Avoid sites that are personal-opinion pieces by people who like to get high. Here are some trustworthy resources:

Books

The Science of Addiction: From Neurobiology to Treatment, by Carlton K. Erickson (New York: W.W. Norton & Company, 2007). This is a detailed but easy-to-understand book on brain science and addiction research.

Marijuana: Facts for Teens, by Barry Leonard (Diane Publishing, 2007). The book gives information about the effects of using marijuana and about addiction.

Websites

Above the Influence
www.abovetheinfluence.com
This is an online resource that provides information about drug abuse, as well as information about resources that you can access. This website is written for teens and provides information to help make decisions about abusing drugs, addiction, and recovery.

KidsHealth
www.kidshealth.org

This website is written by health professionals and has separate sites for parents, kids, and teens. It has information about common side effects of abusing prescription and OTC drugs, signs and symptoms of drug abuse, and what to do if you're worried about yourself or someone you care about.

National Institute on Drug Abuse
www.drugabuse.gov

This government website provides detailed information about classes of drugs, their side effects, symptoms of overdose and withdrawal, and signs and symptoms of drug abuse.

Organizations, Hotlines, and Helplines

Substance Abuse and Mental Health Service Administration (SAMHSA) (1-800-662-HELP)
(www.samhsa.gov)

This agency has a hotline and website and can help you locate treatment centers, help agencies, and counselors in your area. Their hotline operates 24 hours a day, 7 days a week and is staffed by compassionate and knowledgeable professionals who can help you take the first step in getting help.

Narcotics Anonymous
(www.na.org)

This website will give you information about the support systems that are available in your community.

Glossary

amygdala A tiny part of the brain associated with the sense of smell

anesthetics A substance or drug that makes someone insensitive to pain

cannabinoids A group of compounds that are the active parts of cannabis

cartels Groups that set prices, control distribution, and restrict competition on something, including drugs

cerebellum A part of the brain at the back of the skull that coordinates muscle activity

colic Pain in the abdomen

commercially Something grown or sold to make a profit

compounds A mixture of two or more substances

controversial Something that causes disagreement

cultivated To grow plants

dependence Needing or relying on something

derived Something formed, made, or prepared from something else

hemp fiber Fiber extracted from the stem of the hemp plant that is used to make rope, fabric, paper, and fiberboard

hippocampus A part of the brain that is believed to be the center of emotion, memory, and the autonomic nervous system

molecular Relating to molecules, or at a microscopic level

mystique Something that is mysterious, evokes awe, or is secretly powerful, baffling, or impressive

nervous system The nerve tissues that control the activities of the body, brain, and spinal cord; also called the central nervous system

paranoia A mental condition where a person loses touch with reality; it includes extreme fear or delusions, and a mistrust of people and their actions without reason or evidence for justification

PCP A synthetic hallucinogenic drug, sometimes called angel dust

perception The ability to see, hear, or be aware of something

propaganda Misleading, biased, or untrue information that is used to promote or publicize a particular view or opinion

shaman A priest-doctor in certain tribal societies who uses magic to heal the sick and control natural events

tincture A medicine made by dissolving a drug in alcohol

trances Half-conscious states of being that are marked by an absence of response to other things

Index